Great Britain, Egypt, and the Suez Canal Volume Talbot collection of British pamphlets – Primary Source Edition

Francis Egerton

From Ray & Claudine.
Dec 2013.
Best wishes. xx

GREAT BRITAIN, EGYPT,

AND

THE SUEZ CANAL

BY

ADMIRAL THE HON. F. EGERTON, M.P.

W. RATHBONE, M.P.

C. M. NORWOOD, M.P.

London:

CHAPMAN AND HALL, Limited,

11, Henrietta Street.

1884.

EGYPT, THE SUEZ CANAL, AND INDIA.

In the accompanying Papers, we have not touched upon the question of the duties and responsibilities of England in Egypt. We have only attempted to deal with the permanent interests of England, commercial and naval, in Egypt and the Suez Canal, and with their comparative value to England and other countries as a means of transporting produce, soldiers, and stores—a subject on which much ignorance and many misconceptions exist.

F. EGERTON, VICE-ADMIRAL.

W. RATHBONE.

C. M. NORWOOD.

London, *May*, 1884.

GREAT BRITAIN, EGYPT,

AND

THE SUEZ CANAL.

The Naval Aspect.

CONSIDERING the Suez Canal from the point of view of a naval man, I think it clear that England may be drawn into a dangerous position by too great reliance upon it, especially, of course, in the case of a great maritime war, but even in that of war with one maritime Power. And if the Canal is an untrustworthy instrument in case of war, is that a fact which is much to be regretted? I think not. If we accept its untrustworthiness as a fact, and make up our minds to invest, probably a small percentage of what some advisers would have us spend on "strengthening our position in Egypt," on a well-considered increase of our naval forces, and of such appliances at home and abroad as would enable us best to use them, I think the result would be eminently beneficial for England.

Nobody disputes the advantages of the Canal in time of peace, or for such operations as those of the Abyssinian war, involving no international difficulties. But how would it be under the circumstances of war with one or more maritime Powers? Our naval and military authorities would, I think, be justified in great hesitation in trusting the transit of store-ships, troop-ships, or even of small vessels of war, to the dangers of the Mediterranean passage, with its coasts affording *points d'appui* for the torpedo vessels and armed cruisers of an enemy. And still less might they think themselves entitled to venture any considerable expedition into the *culs de sac* either of the Mediterranean or of the Red Sea, in the uncertainty as to whether on arrival at the isthmus it would find its road clear, for I take it as indubitable that the Canal could be blocked if a Power at war with us thought fit to do so. Of course it may be urged that we ought to hold Egypt, or at least so much of it as would ensure our passage. That opens a political question which it is not my business to discuss, but even were we so to decide, and act on the decision, I doubt if even under that condition we could be sure of our ability to secure the passage at all times ; and though, no doubt, whatever might be the means taken for blocking the Canal we could eventually clear it, the danger consists in the suddenness with which the mischief might be done at a critical moment. There is also the minor point that we would be unwilling to use the Canal for warlike purposes, such as the passage of ships of war, on account of the international difficulties which might arise. Our fleet, if only it be made strong enough for the purpose, would be better employed in clearing the seas outside the Canal than in guarding its passage.

F. EGERTON.

The Political and Commercial Aspect.

GREAT BRITAIN AND THE SUEZ CANAL.

(Reprinted from the *Fortnightly Review*, August, 1882.)

AT this moment the attention of all Europe is fixed upon the course of events in Egypt. The Egyptian policy of our Government, a matter of deep interest to all the great States of Europe, is doubly interesting to us, the citizens of the United Kingdom. Men entertain different opinions as to what that policy should be, but each would justify his opinion by referring to the vital interests of our Empire in the East. One question has been hotly discussed, the question whether any special interest of England, apart from the rest of Europe, binds us to follow the perilous course entered on by Lord Salisbury, to continue his co-partnership with France in the management of Egyptian affairs, a course leading to impossible positions, a co-partnership dangerous to international amity; or whether we are free to carry out a policy which, in the hands of the Liberal Government, has elsewhere proved so successful, the policy of settling those affairs in concert with the other Powers of Europe, who are equally interested in them. The latter seems to me the calm, dignified policy of a nation strong in its own position and in the consciousness of its own power; the former seems the fussy and timorous policy of a Government afraid of everybody, and, therefore, meddling with everything.

Most people seem to believe that we have in Egypt a vital interest which we are bound, more than other nations, to defend, in the free and unrestricted use of the Suez Canal. Few seem disposed to question the doctrine that the open passage through the Suez Canal is indispensable to the commercial prosperity, to the political greatness, and to the very integrity of the British Empire.

An attempt, then, to demonstrate the fallacy of the popular idea that through Egypt and the Suez Canal our enemies can strike at our mercantile greatness and at our imperial power, is not likely to meet with a favourable hearing. Yet I hope to show this, and illustrate it from my own personal experience. And if it can be done, it is worth trying to do it. For it is of the utmost consequence that we should all understand our real stake in the Suez Canal. This once clearly understood, we shall not be liable to panic; we shall not let ourselves be drawn into complications, wasteful of the blood of our citizens and the substance of our country; complications, moreover, which constantly expose us to the danger of becoming involved in a European war.

I do not for a moment wish to depreciate the enormous

advantage which the Suez Canal has conferred upon producers and consumers both in Asia and in Europe, upon our fellow-subjects in India, and upon our own people at home. The Suez Canal is one of the noblest works of modern enterprise and modern science, and I regret that any English statesman should have opposed its construction. It has been of the utmost value to the general commerce of the world. Its maintenance is, in this sense, an interest common to all nations, and especially to all commercial nations. But when people attempt to make out that the formation of the Suez Canal has in any way promoted our commercial preponderance, or that our commercial preponderance could be destroyed by its destruction, or that we are any longer dependent on it for the rapid transfer of men and material of war from England to India, it can be shown from the actual results which have attended the opening of the Canal, from the history of commerce, and from the present power of our commercial marine, that they are mistaken. The Suez Canal has not improved the commercial position of England relatively to that of other Powers; it has done just the contrary. Let us ask, What are already the established results of this great work?

Let us take a most important trade, the business of supplying East India cotton to the manufacturers of the Continent. I will give the history of East India cotton intended for the supply of a, say, Austrian manufacturer some forty years ago and at the present time. At that time cotton came down from the interior of India on bullock-carts, each cart carrying four bales. A native merchant, generally a Parsee, collected and assorted the cotton, and shipped it under advances from an English merchant in Bombay, who charged 2½ per cent. for so doing. It was carried by an English wooden sailing ship to England, consigned to an English merchant in Liverpool or London, who stored it in an English warehouse, insured it with an English assurance company, and sold it with a commission of 2½ per cent. to another Liverpool or London merchant. The latter purchased it under orders for, say, an Austrian manufacturer, to whom he charged a further commission of 2 per cent. for his trouble. Each of these merchants received thus a handsome commission, and the English warehouse owner, assurance company, and labourer were in turn paid for their services. Then the cotton was shipped on an English sailing ship or steam-vessel for Trieste, whence it was finally forwarded for the manu-facturer's use.

Now all these operations, profitable to English mer-chants, shipowners, labourers, and others, have in most cases ceased; and the Austrian manufacturer can and does contract with a Bombay house through its European agent for the shipment direct from Bombay to Trieste of the required bales of cotton. Some of this cotton, it is true, is still carried by an English ship, but for a much shorter distance and for a small fraction of the freight formerly charged. I need not add that even for this fragment of the old traffic the energetic Mediterranean shipowner competes severely with the shipowner of our own country. For the Mediterranean shipowner has the advantage of being present in person at one end of the voyage to watch with a master's eye the disbursements, the condition of his vessels, and the conduct and management of his captains and his crews.

What has been said of our Austrian competitor holds no less true of all our other competitors on the Continent. What has happened in the cotton trade has happened in other trades. Tea, for instance, now comes direct from China to Russia. In my early days London was the centre of the Eastern silk trade. The silk of China and of India came to London, and was thence distributed over Europe. Formerly this was one of the most profitable branches of our business. Since the opening of the Suez Canal, Lyons has succeeded London as the capital market for the silk of the East. But, with regard to silk, the Suez Canal perhaps did no more than assist a process already begun. Being so valuable an article, it was, to a considerable extent, brought across the Isthmus previous to the opening of the Canal. What Trieste and Lyons have gained at the expense of London and Liverpool, that Havre, Marseilles, and Odessa have gained too. To complain of all this would be ridiculous. That it should be so

B

is perfectly right. But it is also ridiculous to say in the face of these facts that the opening of the Suez Canal has specially benefited the commercial interests of England as compared with other nations. On the contrary, it has favoured those nations at our expense, and the freedom of the Canal means more to them than it does to us.

It would be most unfair, however, to attribute exclusively to the Suez Canal the disappearance of so many intermediate agencies between the Indian producer and the European consumer. At the present day there is in all trades a tendency to bring the producer and the consumer into more immediate connection. But what the Suez Canal has done is to stimulate and accelerate this tendency, and to transfer the remaining agency between producer and consumer from England, once the centre and depôt of the commerce between Asia and Europe, to the ports and cities of the Mediterranean.

A short historical retrospect will place this matter in a clearer light, and may serve to show that the changes in commerce which have followed upon the opening of the Suez Canal are not accidental or irregular, but are rather the first effects of causes which will operate in the future constantly and with accumulated force.

The opening of the Suez Canal has exactly reversed what took place when the route round the Cape of Good Hope was substituted for the overland routes between Europe and the East. These overland routes in the fourteenth century seem to have been principally three. One of these routes passed through Egypt; another ran through Bagdad and Tabreez to the ports of Antioch and Seleucia; whilst the third traversed the highlands of Armenia and terminated at Trebizond. Western Asia, although it had declined from its former prosperity, was still rich, populous, and fairly well culti- vated. Alexandria was then, what it has become once more, a great emporium of Oriental merchandise, and Constantinople was not inferior to Alexandria. From the ports of Egypt and Asia Minor that merchandise passed over to the West in the ships of Venice and Genoa. From those cities it was distributed through the Alpine passes to the Free Cities of Southern Germany and the Rhine. In bulk, variety, and value, it was insignificant indeed compared with the cargoes that now pass through the Suez Canal. Yet how many German and Italian cities owed to this toilsome Oriental traffic their wealth and magnificence? Professor Thorold Rogers brings this out clearly in his most interesting book on the "History of Agriculture and Prices in England." He says: "In the fifteenth century such towns as Nuremberg and Ratisbon, Mayence and Cologne, were at the height of their opulence. The waterway of the Rhine bears ineffaceable traces of the wealth which was carried down it in the numerous castles of the robber barons, the extirpation of whom became the first object to which the resources of civilisation were directed. The trade of the East enriched the burghers of the Low Countries, till, after a long and tedious transit, the abundant spices of the East, increased in price a hundredfold by the tolls which rapacity exacted and the profits which merchants imposed, were sold in small parcels by the grocer or apothecary, or purchased in larger quantities by wealthy consumers, at the great fair of Stourbridge or in the perpetual market of London " (Vol. iv., p. 654).

Then came a memorable revolution. Western Asia was repeatedly ravaged by the Turkish and Tartar hordes. In many rich, fertile, and famous countries the cultivated lands returned to their primitive desolation ; great cities shrank into miserable country towns, and the people sank into an incurable and hopeless lethargy. The Christian merchant found it more and more dangerous, less and less profitable, to penetrate into the interior of Asia. At length the Turkish conquerors reached the Bosphorus and the Hellespont. The Greek Emperors gave place to the Ottoman Sultans, and under their new masters the Euxine and Asia Minor were closed to Christian commerce. From Constantinople the Ottomans spread their conquests to the Danube on the one side, and the Euphrates on the other. Finally Selim I. subdued Mesopotamia, the holy cities of Arabia, and Egypt, and stopped the last overland route a few years after Vasco de Gama had discovered the passage round the

Cape of Good Hope. Professor Thorold Rogers has shown with great fulness how Selim's conquest of Egypt raised the price of almost every Oriental commodity imported into Europe. The same conquest struck a fatal blow at the greatness of many an Italian and German city. From this epoch we may date the decline of Venice, and Venice scarcely suffered more than Ratisbon, Augsburg, and Nuremberg. There, for generations, many an untenanted palace, many a silent street, reminded the traveller of that great change in the line of Eastern commerce.

Then Portugal first, and afterwards England and Holland, seized on the sea route to India, and on the traffic of the East. England, who added to that rich monopoly the Empire of India and of the seas, was to Europe all that Venice and Genoa, Augsburg and Nuremberg, had been; and she was much more. But the decline of the Ottoman Empire, followed by the construction of the Suez Canal and of the Alpine tunnels, has reopened the old path of commerce. The cities of the Mediterranean are reviving. The Mediterranean States have gained much and we have lost something, even in the last few years; and as time goes on they will continue to gain and we to lose. Any one who visited, as I did, the cities of Southern Europe forty years ago, then cities of the dead, would hardly recognise them now—all bustle, activity, and progress. But we must not forget that political freedom has had as much effect as the return of Eastern commerce in the renewal of their prosperity.

The English merchant is not so selfish as to complain of a change which has benefited the producers and consumers of the world. Instead of sitting down with his hands before him, bemoaning his hard fate or living upon a reduced trade, he has, as I shall indicate later on, found out new trades, if not so profitable to individuals even more beneficial to mankind than those which he has lost.

We shall be told, perhaps, to look at the immense increase in the mercantile marine of England. That increase has really had quite other causes. The invention of the compound steam-engine, which effected an enormous saving of fuel, took place shortly before the opening of the Suez Canal. One leaf out of the experience of our own firm will serve to exemplify how completely the carrying trade of the world was transformed by this invention. A few years before the opening of the Suez Canal we built and fitted with the new compound engines a steamer intended for the Alexandria trade. On her first voyage we found that, with a consumption of fuel less by one-third, she carried five hundred tons more of cargo than a steamer previously built for the same trade. Such an economy of fuel in proportion to cargo at once pointed to a revolution in the carrying trade. It meant that in future all valuable cargoes, at least, would be carried in iron steamers, not as formerly, in wooden sailing ships.

Since the abolition of the Navigation Laws no ship-owners in the world have been more energetic or enter-prising than the British. Great Britain is the greatest iron shipbuilding yard, and also the most active machine-shop, in the world. London is the world's financial capital. To a vigorous use of these advantages, and not to the construc-tion of the Suez Canal, this country owes the unrivalled development of her carrying trade. She has lost the large profits derived from her former position as geographical centre of the trade between Asia and Europe, but she has found fresh trades and fresh industries. Instead of bringing to England cotton and silk from India and China to be distributed over Europe, she brings millions of quarters of grain grown by her subjects in India to feed her artisans at home. Up to the present time she has even held her own in the carrying trade between her Indian possessions and the ports of the Mediterranean. Her merchants have now lost many large profits once realised by them, but she now has far more manufacturers, merchants, and other traders who make moderate incomes. Her political freedom, her freedom of trade, her enormous capital, the energy, enterprise, and experience of her citizens, have averted the fate which in similar circum-stances overtook the great marts of mediæval commerce. And those beneficent Powers will continue to avert that fate so long as her manufacturers, merchants, and other tradesmen retain their enterprise and integrity, her mechanical engineers their inventive skill, her artisans their intelligence and industry. To these good qualities, and to these fortunate circumstances, but not to the making of the Suez Canal, she will owe her mercantile prosperity. Had the Canal never been made she would have maintained that prosperity as fully and with less effort. It is, therefore, as absurd for us to say, as it is undesirable for foreigners to believe, that by closing the Canal they can ruin the commerce of the United Kingdom.

Then as to the necessity to England of the Suez Canal for the swift transport of men and munitions of war to India, it would be most valuable, no doubt, in case of mutiny in India unaccompanied by a European war. But in case of any war in which a Mediterranean State was concerned, I do not for a moment believe that the Canal would be available. On this subject I would refer to Mr. Caine's letter in the *Daily News*, and to Mr. Norwood's full and carefully written letter to the *Times* of the 10th of July. In confirmation thereof I am advised that there would be no difficulty in building transports capable of performing the journey to Bombay by way of the Cape in about thirty-one days, only four days more than the time occupied by the steamers of the Peninsular and Oriental Company in reaching the same destination by way of the Canal. Our present troopships, I believe, perform the shorter voyage in about thirty-one days. The improved troopships would perform the voyage through the Canal in shorter time, if no danger or impediment lay in their course. But if we were at war with a Mediterranean Power, they would be exposed to such dangers in passing an enemy's shores through those narrow seas, they would be so much harassed by gunboats and torpedo-vessels issuing from the enemy's ports, that they would probably have to be placed under convoys, which would counteract in point of speed any advantage to be gained in going through the Canal. On the other hand, while we control the high seas, such swift and powerful transports would be dangerous to follow and difficult to capture in mid-ocean, where our cruisers would outnumber the cruisers of the enemy, and our ports of refuge would be nearer than theirs.

These arguments seem to me to have a conclusive bearing on our present position. It is not necessary for the protection of our commerce, it is not essential to our communication with India, that we should entangle ourselves in a partnership with any single State in Europe for the protection of peculiarly English interests. Surely the present Government were amply justified in hesitating to intervene in Egypt, in alliance with a single Power, at any rate, before asking, in the first instance, for the help of a European concert. I hope that they will take the first opportunity of liberating themselves altogether from the false system engendered by the suspicious fears of their predecessors, by a timidity which led to alternate displays of rashness and weakness. Such partnerships can lead us in the future only where they have led us in the past, into positions which no Government, however able or well-disposed, can maintain with credit or escape from without either national misunderstandings or the sacrifice of British wealth and British lives. That which is really a European interest should be provided for by European concert. Our experience in the Crimea might have prevented the late Government from entering on such a course in conjunction with a country whose policy was, and still is, in a state of constant change and uncertainty.

WILLIAM RATHBONE.

P.S.—*May*, 1884. The following passages, taken from an article by Mr. Gladstone, which appeared in the "Nineteenth Century" (No. 6), for August, 1877, put the permanent interests of England in this question so clearly that they will be read with interest now :—

Lastly, that I myself approach the question (Mr. Dicey's proposal that England should take possession of the Delta of Egypt) under adverse prepossessions. It is my firm conviction, derived, I think, from my political 'pastors and masters,' and confirmed by the facts of much experience, that, as a general rule, enlargements of the Empire are for us an evil fraught with serious, though possibly not with immediate danger. I do not affirm that they can always be avoided ; but, that they should never be accepted except under circumstances of a strict and jealously examined necessity. I object to them because they are rarely effected except by means that are more or less questionable, and that tend to compromise British character in the judgment of the impartial world ; a judgment, which I hope will grow from age to age more and more operative in imposing moral restraint on the proceedings of each particular State. I object to them, because we already have our hands too full. We have undertaken responsibilities of government such as never were assumed before in the whole history of the world. The cares of the governing body in the Roman Empire, with its compact continuity of ground, were light in comparison with the demands now made upon the Parliament and Executive of the United Kingdom. Claims made, and gallantly, or confidently at least, confronted, yet not adequately met. We, who hail with more than readiness annexations and other transactions which extend and complicate our responsibilities abroad, who are always ready for a new task, yet leave many of the old tasks undone. Forty years have passed since it was thought right to reform fundamentally our municipal corporations ; but the Corporation of London, whose case called out for change much more loudly than any other, we have not yet had time or strength to touch. Our currency, our local government, our liquor laws, portions even of our taxation, remain in a state either positively discreditable, or at the least inviting and demanding great improvement ; but, for want of time and strength, we cannot handle them. For the romance of political travel we are ready to scour the world, and yet of capital defect in duties lying at our door we are not ashamed.

I protest upon another ground, which, if not more broad and solid than the two foregoing grounds, is yet at least more palpable. The most pacific of prudent men must keep in his view the leading outlines of the condition which we shall have to accept in future wars. As regards the strength, the spirit, the resources of the country, we have nothing to fear. Largely dependent at other times on timber, hemp, and metal of foreign origin for the construction of our navy, we now find ourselves constituted, by the great transition from wooden to iron ships, the principal producers of the one indispensable raw material, and the first ship manufacturers of the world. But one subject remains, which fills me with a real alarm. It is the fewness of our men. Ample in numbers to defend our island-home, they are, with reference to the boundless calls of our world-wide dominion, but as a few grains of sand scattered thinly on a floor. Men talk of humiliation: may we never be subjected to the humiliation of dependence upon vicarious valour, bought dear and sold cheap in the open market. Public extravagance does not with us take the humour of overpay to our soldiers and our sailors. In war time, we must ungrudgingly add (and it is no easy matter) to the emoluments of the services. But after we have done all that is possible, we shall not have done enough. It will still remain an effort beyond, and almost against, Nature, for some thirty millions of men to bear in chief the burden of defending the countries inhabited by near three hundred millions. We must not flinch from the performance of our duty to those countries. But neither let us, by puerile expedients, try to hide from ourselves what it involves. To divest ourselves of territory once acquired is very difficult. Where it is dishonourable, it cannot be thought of. Even where it is not, it is likely to set in action some reasonable as well as many unreasonable susceptibilities. If then we commit an error in adding to territory, it is an error impossible or difficult to cure. It fills me with surprise that the disproportion between our population and our probable duties in war is so little felt, especially (so far as I know) by professional men, as a prudential restraint upon the thirst of more territory. The surrender of the Ionian

Protectorate was not founded on a desire to husband our military means ; but, even as estimated by that result, it was one of the very best measures of our time. Pp. 151, 152.

* * * * *

Again, on page 158 :

Reverting to Egypt, I observe that Mr. Dicey dwells on the smallness of the territory. This smallness, he says, makes it absolutely impossible for two rival Governments to be within its limits. He proposes, however, all along, that we shall have, as far as it reaches locally, a supreme control in Governments; for we are to hold secure military possession, to keep down the taxes, and to check oppression. Yet he also proposes that the sphere of our commanding influence is to be confined to the Delta. There appear to be here some inconsistencies. Of what use is military command within the Delta for the custody of the Canal ? And is not the dualism of Government, once renounced, also resumed ? But I am not acting as a critic. What I seek to impress is, that territorial questions are not to be disposed of by arbitrary limits ; that we cannot enjoy the luxury of taking Egyptian soil by pinches. We may seize an Aden and a Perim, where there is no already formed community of inhabitants, and circumscribe a tract at will. But our first site in Egypt, be it by larceny or be it by emption, will be the almost certain egg of a North African Empire, that will grow and grow until another Victoria and another Albert, titles of the lake-sources of the White Nile, come within our borders ; and till we finally join hands across the Equator with Natal and Cape Town, to say nothing of the Transvaal and the Orange River on the south, or of

Abyssinia or Zanzibar to be swallowed by way of viaticum on our journey. And then, with a great empire in each of the four quarters of the world, and with the whole new or fifth quarter to ourselves, we may be territorially content, but less than ever at our ease; for if agitators and alarmists can now find at almost every spot 'British interests' to bewilder and disquiet us, their quest will then be all the wider, in proportion as the excepted points will be the fewer.

Egypt proper is indeed a small country. Our most recent and most comprehensive informant, Mr. M'Coan, fixing its boundary at the First Cataract, points out that the French, in 1798, found a cultivable surface of only 9,600 square miles, since extended to 11,350. It cannot be allowable to suppose one portion of this tract under our supreme controlling authority, and another free from it. Moreover, it is vain to disguise that we shall have the entire responsibility of the government, if we have any of it at all. Mr. Dicey says we must prevent intolerable oppression. I hold that we shall have to deal with all oppression, tolerable or not; and therefore and beyond all things with the entire taxation of the country, which is the fountain-head of the oppression, both tolerable and intolerable. In an Egypt controlled and developed by us, every detail of the popular life and state will be familiar to the English and the European eye. It will not be shielded by remoteness, as is even now the interior of our Indian communities; it is nowhere, so to speak, out of sight of the Nile. We cannot, as in our free colonies, divest ourselves of direct responsibility through the gift of self-government. If we could, the problem, simplified in one aspect, would be complicated in another; for who can say what would be the opinion of a self-governing Egypt on the question whether it would go to seek a master in the British Isles, or whether it would prefer an independent domesticated ruler, identified with its religion, not alien to its race, and rooted already by blood in the recent traditions of its resurrection and its growth? Be it the Foreign Secretary, or be it the Colonial Secretary, or be it an Egyptian Secretary of State, manufactured *ad hoc*, I cannot envy him his prospective charge: and though he would give certainty and finality (as the Russians everywhere do) to the abolition of slavery, and would import a multitude of improvements under the eye of our Parliament, and stimulated by its interpellations and debates, I am far from being entirely sure that the action of our popular system might not prove greatly too vivid and direct to please the sheiks and the fellaheen, even while it might profit them.

* * * * *

And again, on page 160:

Viewing all these facts, I, for one, am inclined, on prudential grounds, to say, ' Hands off.'

But if this be so with reference to the confined area of Egypt proper, much more must we be moved to abstain when we consider that Egypt proper is not alone in question. The rulers of a narrow country have striven hard to extend their authority over a space proportioned to its primeval dignity, and to the day when it contended with Assyria for the empire of the world. From the seat of their recognised dominion, they have directed the eye and stretched out the arm over all Nubia to Dongola, and beyond it into the Beled-es-Soudan, or Country of the Blacks, which reaches without a boundary away beyond Abyssinia, and as far as the frontier of Zanzibar. It is a territory, says M'Coan, five times larger than that ruled by the Pharaohs, the Ptolemies, and the Caliphs; for administrative purposes it already touches Gondokoro; and a glance at the map will show that from this point to the Mediterranean we have a reach of nearly 2,000 miles, with an area, according to M'Coan, more than twice that of the Austrian Empire. The population of Egypt proper approaches six millions, and that of Nubia and the Upper Nile is taken at ten to eleven millions. Now, as relations of some kind have been contracted by the Khedive with this vast region and large population, the questions must press upon us with relentless force, first, whether, to protect a few score miles of canal, we are to take the charge of 2000 miles of territory; and if not, then, secondly, at what point and by what process we are to quash the relations of superiority and subordination already formed, and to repudiate the obligations they entail?

The Aspects of the Question as altered by Improvements in Steam Navigation.

THE SUEZ CANAL.

To the Editor of " The Times."

SIR,

In the debate on Mr. Chaplin's motion for the adjournment of the House, on the 22nd ult., I expressed the opinion that the popular estimate as to the vital importance of the Suez Canal, especially with reference to our hold upon India, is much exaggerated; and I cited the remarkable progress made in marine engineering the past year or two, as having materially reduced the advantage hitherto possessed by the Canal over the Cape route. The importance, at the present moment, of a correct appreciation of our position in reference to this question, induces me to ask your permission to state my views in some detail, though I shall do so as concisely as I can.

Of the great commercial convenience of the Canal route, especially to Indian ports, there can be but one opinion. The large saving it effects will be seen by the following statement of comparative distances from London, in nautical miles :—

	Via Canal.	*Via* Cape.
Bombay	6,330	10,595
Madras	7,330	10,830
Calcutta	7,950	11,450
Singapore	8,345	11,670

This route has the further advantage of frequent ports of call where bunkers can be replenished—viz. Gibraltar, Malta, Port Said, Aden, and Colombo, which enables steamers of comparatively small size and power to convey cargoes at a *minimum* cost. The result has been a vast increase in our steam tonnage, and a diversion to the Canal route of the great bulk of our Eastern traffic, so that of the total tonnage passing the Canal in 1881—4,143,683 tons—British merchant shipping represents no less than 3,371,058 tons. Our relief troopships and other Government vessels also used the Canal to the extent of 72,126 tons. The time occupied at present by the Peninsular and Oriental Company's steamers from Gravesend to Bombay is 27 days, to Madras 33 days, and to Calcutta 37 days, and their steaming is about 11 knots. The British India Company's steamers are timed to make the passage to Calcutta, calling at Colombo and Madras, in 40 days: but the average speed of the ordinary cargo boats using the Canal does not exceed a continuous steaming of 9 knots, and the length of the passages made by them is proportionately increased.

Our troopships, I estimate, will occupy fully 10 per cent. more time than the P. and O. service above referred to.

The question of interest, as it seems to me in the present condition of affairs in Egypt, is this: Assuming that the Canal be no longer available to our merchant steamers and transports, what would be the effect on our national interests? My reply is, that the dislocation of existing arrangements would entail considerable inconvenience and loss upon individuals. Bombay would lose much of the importance she now possesses from her position on the west coast—the conveyance of merchandise would occupy a longer period, and rates of freight, at the outset especially, would be somewhat enhanced—though there would be a partial set-off against the increased consumption of fuel, wages and interest on capital, in the saving of the heavy toll levied by the Canal, amounting (with pilotage and light dues) to nearly 11s. per net registered ton. It should not be forgotten that the average time occupied in the passage is two days, and it occasionally happens that a delay of three or four days arises from the grounding of vessels in the Canal.

In my opinion, however, the inconvenience and loss just named would not be of any serious or permanent character; traffic would adjust itself to the altered circumstance with marvellous rapidity; and there can be no question that our existing mercantile marine and our building yards were never so capable of responding to the call that would be made upon them.

We possess a fine fleet of sailing vessels, a portion of which is now employed in the conveyance of India produce by the Cape. Their number could be readily increased by a transfer from the Australian trades, which are not at present very profitable.

The more bulky and less costly products of India, such as grain and seed, and the coal and iron exported from hence do not require very rapid conveyance; and it not unfrequently happens that lastage by sailing vessels is quoted in Calcutta at the same rate as by ordinary cargo steamers. The smaller and less powerful steamers now using the Canal would probably be transferred to other trades; but by far the greater number are competent to perform the passage (calling at the Cape, and, if needful, at St. Vincent); and they would be reinforced by the unprecedentedly large number of cargo steamers of large carrying capacity now being constructed for private owners with a primary view to the American grain trade.

The amount of tonnage now in process of construction, under Lloyd's supervision, is considerably upwards of 1,000,000 tons. Passengers and valuable merchandise would continue to be conveyed by the Peninsular and

Oriental Company, the British India, the Ducal, and other lines; and it must not be overlooked that the Union and Donald Currie Companies carry on a regular and efficient service to the Cape, which might readily be extended to India. All these companies have recently added powerful new vessels to their fleets, and it is probable that the Peninsular and Oriental Company's boats, the *Rome* and the *Carthage*, of 5,013 tons gross and 5,000 effective horse-power, and the *Ballarat* and *Parramatta*, of 4,700 tons gross and 4,000 effective horse-power, now building, would make the passage in about 36 days to Bombay, and 38 or 39 days to Calcutta, including coaling at the Cape.

There yet remain to be added to the list of our resources the very important fleet of Transatlantic steamers belonging to Liverpool, capable of steaming 14 or 16 knots, to some of which recourse could be had in case of need, and also the supply of new and improved vessels which our building yards are capable of producing within a comparatively short period. This brings me to the most important national consideration involved in the closing of the Canal, and that to which I specially referred in my remarks in the House—viz., the conveyance of mails and troops.

The mail and express passenger service to India is performed now, as it was prior to the construction of the Canal, by express trains to Brindisi, thence by steamer to Alexandria, joining the Peninsular and Oriental boat at Suez, and reaching Bombay in 18 days from London.

This service is not in any way dependent on the Canal, and can be carried on with the assent of the *de facto* Government of Egypt for the time being (and providing that there is no political obstacle to the passage over the Continent to and from Brindisi), even should the passage of the Canal be closed.

The movement for an accelerated packet service to the United States, originated by the construction of the steamship *Arizona* by Messrs. John Elder and Co., of Glasgow, for the Guion line in 1879, has led to the production, within the past twelve months, of ocean steamships of a size and speed previously unknown ; and through the enterprise of Liverpool owners, carried into effect by the skill of naval architects and engineers on the banks of the Clyde, the practicability of continuous ocean steaming of 17 and even 18 knots per hour is placed beyond dispute.

It may seem invidious to single out two or three from the many fine steamers recently acquired by our great companies, but to illustrate my meaning I will instance the *Alaska*, of the Guion line, built by Elders, 6,932 tons gross; *Servia*, of the Cunard line, built by Thomson, 7,392 tons gross; *City of Rome*, of the Inman line, built by Barrow Company, 8,415 tons gross.

I have before me the particulars of the *Alaska's* performances. Her last voyage from Sandy Hook to Queenstown was made in 6 days 22 hours, and from Queenstown in 7 days 2 hours, or a continuous speed of upwards of 400 nautical miles per day. It is no secret, I believe, that the builders of the *Alaska* are constructing a vessel to eclipse even her performances. The *Oregon* is to be 500 feet between perpendiculars, 54 feet beam, and about 40 feet moulded depth, indicated H.P. 13,000; consumption about 220 tons per day on very full steaming, and, with 20 days' coal supply, she will have large capacity for troops, horses, stores, &c. Should the *Oregon*, like her elder sisters, the *Arizona* and *Alaska*, fulfil in practice the anticipation of her constructors, she would be able to carry troops from Plymouth to Bombay in 24 days, and to Calcutta in about 26 days, allowing for coaling at the Cape, which experience has shown can be effected at the rate of about 120 tons per hour. This would be considerably less time than is now occupied by Her Majesty's transports, or the P. and O. Company's service, *viâ* the Canal, and only a week more than the Overland Mail.

Vessels of this class are necessarily costly to construct and expensive to work. For mercantile purposes they could be remunerative only on a passenger line of importance, or when aided by a postal subsidy, and it is not to be expected that private individuals would venture on the outlay on a mere chance of eventualities, more or less remote. But the acquisition of a fleet of highly-powered transports, in addition to, or in substitution for, the obsolete vessels we now possess (which have done excellently good service in their day), would be a wise provision on the part of our Government, and could be effected at an expenditure which would be a bagatelle in comparison with the sense of relief from the international complications and difficulties (and possible waste of blood and treasure) to which an exaggerated estimate of the value of the Canal exposes us. England won her Indian Empire and conducted her vast commerce until 1869 by the great ocean highway; and I am convinced that, with reasonable precautions, she is now equally able to retain them by the same route.

I need scarcely add that the saving of distance by the Canal is lessened to ports to the eastward of Singapore, until at Melbourne the distance from England is the same by either route.

Your obedient Servant,

C. M. NORWOOD.

House of Commons, *July 5th*, 1882.

CHARLES DICKENS AND EVANS, CRYSTAL PALACE PRESS.

Lightning Source UK Ltd.
Milton Keynes UK
UKOW02f2130101213

222776UK00007B/291/P